Presented to

_____

By

_____

book of christian prayer

+

Leslie F. brandt

AUGSBURG Publishing House • Minneapolis

BOOK OF CHRISTIAN PRAYER

LCCC 73-88603   ISBN 0-8066-1406-4

Manufactured in the U.S.A.   APH 10-0785

0 1 2 3 4 5 6 7 8 9

CONTENTS

FOR SPECIAL PEOPLE

MY RELATIONSHIP WITH GOD

PRAISE AND THANKS

NATION AND WORLD

IN THE EVENING

PREFACE

I profess no expertise in writing prayers. I just know that I have feelings, some that cannot be expressed in words, others that explode in honest, agonizing, remorseful, or grateful expressions. My prayers are personal talks with God in everyday words, a language I find more meaningful than the formal prayer language which served us well in years past.

I have previously written and published the contemporary psalms which, I believe, reflect what ancient psalmists might have expressed had they lived in our century. This *Book of Christian Prayer* is a sampling of how 20th-century Christians might verbalize their feelings in conversations with God.

These prayers are honest attempts to express the human condition in a variety of situations. If they encourage or assist others to discover the joy and freedom of being open and honest before God, I shall be grateful.

I want to express my gratitude to my editors for suggestions and encouragement, and to my wife, Edith, who lovingly rounds off the rough edges of both the author and his books.

LESLIE F. BRANDT

IN THE MORNING

WHAT I WANT
FOR TODAY

You've granted me another day, O Lord.
Yesterday with its wasted opportunities
and selfish enterprises is gone forever.
I don't suppose today will be much different, Lord.
But it could be, if I stay within your orbit for my life
and run your errands
and recognize my appointment and commitment
as your servant within this fractured world.
So be it, Lord.
It is what I want, Lord.
Because of me, or in spite of me,
may your love touch some lonely, needy person
today.
I no longer want to build empires,
to ascend thrones,
or to be number one in my little kingdom.
I want to love you,
and to respond to your love for me
by communicating such love to others.
This is what I want, O Lord,
but you know my soft spots, my hang-ups.
May the victory be yours today, O Lord.

THANKS
FOR ANOTHER DAY

Thank you, my loving God, for another day.
I don't know what adventures it holds for me.
I may be surprised by joy,
or wounded by pain or sorrow.
Help me to be thankful in all circumstances,
to really believe that what comes my way
comes by way of your loving will and permission.
Grant, O God, that I meet it as your child,
without doubt or fear,
to know that whatever happens,
my relationship to you is never in jeopardy.
And grant that I may be able
to bring your love and joy
into the difficult circumstances that confront me.

WHEN THE WORLD
LOOKS OMINOUS

The world looks ominous today, O Lord.
I am reluctant to leave my warm bed,
the security of my home,
to brave the elements of nature
and the distortions of this human race.
I just don't feel that I have what it takes
to live as you would have me to live
amid the pains and problems of your people
around me.
I am afraid, Lord, and I am ashamed.
Give me courage, O God.
You do not require that I win every battle,
just that I pick up my arms—or my cross—
and enter into the arena of life.
You are not asking me to fret or fuss
over the insurmountable circumstances
that confront me,
just that I be myself—
your son, your disciple, your representative—
and to reach out to others in love,
to help share or bear another's burdens,
to allow your Spirit to work out your will
through me.
So I go forth, my great God,
by your orders, and in your power.
Have it your way, O Lord, in me and through me.

A PROBLEM THAT PERSISTS

I've long had this problem, Lord,
this pernicious little demon
that keeps disturbing my peace of mind.
Maybe you permit it
to hover around the fringes in my life
to drive me incessantly to your fountain of grace.
More likely it is my own little pet
I want to keep out of sight
but not out of consciousness.
It may even be a part of my God-given mortality
which I can't shuck
until I shuck this body itself.
Keep it, O Lord, from coming
between me and you today,
and keep it from hurting
my brothers and sisters about me.
And thank you, Lord,
for accepting and loving
and using me just as I am,
and for persisting in drawing me
toward what you want me to be.

SOMETHING
I MUST FACE TODAY

I should be grateful for a new day, Lord,
especially after a sleepless night.
But I'm not.
There's something I must face today,
and it scares me even to think about it.
You have said that I need never be afraid
if I walk in your footsteps.
You have promised that all things
will work out for good for those who follow you.
You have challenged me to live
joyfully and thankfully
whatever the circumstances that crowd me.
Help me to get my values in order, O God,
to measure my progress by your perspectives,
to gauge my success by your measurements.
O God, help me to trust you,
even if I appear to make no progress whatsoever
or fail in what I propose to do.
My life is yours, O Lord,
and so is this day before me.
I submit the coming hours into your hands
and pray that your Spirit may guide me
through this dark tunnel of doubt,
and if it be your will,
enable me to break into the bright sunlight
of victory at the other end.

ANOTHER DAY OF WAITING

O God, so much of life is wasted in waiting:
for a dear one to return home,
for a letter from a lover,
for news about a friend who is very ill,
for a paycheck to sustain my bodily needs.
The dawn of a new day is the dawn of another day
of marking time, of hoping, longing, and aching.
Teach me, dear God, how to turn the days of waiting
into days of opportunity:
to pray for someone who is ill,
to write to someone who is lonely,
to demonstrate concern for someone who suffers,
to speak lovingly with someone
who is afraid or angry.
Help me today to be less concerned
about my needs and wants,
or about those things
that I cannot control or make happen,
and help me touch someone with love.
Then this day will be a great day,
and it will not be wasted in waiting.

TEACH ME
HOW TO SOAR

This is your day, O Lord.
You made it; it belongs to you.
And yet you share it with me
with all of its opportunities and challenges,
its problems and its risks.
I thank you for your day, O Lord,
and for whatever it may bring my way.
Keep me from becoming entrapped in its snares
or tripped up by its pitfalls,
its corruptions and larcenies.
Teach me how to soar, my God.
Even while I labor in the valley,
may I float free above the cloud-shrouded,
snow-capped peaks that hover over its edges.
And let me be free to set others free,
to introduce some brother or sister
to that glorious release, that life of soaring,
that is made possible for those
who are reconciled to you.
This is your day, O Lord,
help me to live it
according to your plan for my life.

FOR MY WORK

STAY WITH ME, LORD

I pray, O Lord,
that being your servant
may always be the primary vocation of my life.
Help me to find some measure of joy
in my labors today,
and to manifest joy
in my personal relationships.
Above all, enable me to be faithful to you
whatever the circumstances that close in about me.
I am yours, dear Lord;
never leave my side.
Stay with me, Lord;
stay with me.

COURAGE TO DO
HARD THINGS

O God, I don't find much contentment in my job.
It is so difficult to believe
that this is your will for my life.
Grant me the courage and the strength
to do the hard things today
and to do them well.
I am going to face things
that I can't handle by myself.
I know the promises concerning your presence,
but help me to feel something of that presence
in the difficult hours of this day.

SUCCESS
IS NOT NECESSARILY IMPORTANT

I thank you, O Lord,
that you love and accept me as I am
and not for what I might accomplish today.
Help me to accept myself as you accept me,
to face this day's problems and challenges
as your child and servant.
It is not so important that I be successful,
but that I be faithful,
that I belong to you
and that I represent and glorify you.
It is important, O God,
that I allow you to have your way
in and through me.
So be it, Lord.

MY ARENA OF SERVICE

I am grateful, my loving God,
for my arena of service,
for a place to put my feet,
for wheels to shoulder and burdens to carry
and lives to touch
in the course of my daily labors.
May I be sensitive to your leading
and to the hurts and needs of people around me.
I step into this day as your messenger and servant.
Help me to be bold yet full of understanding,
steeped in conviction while humble and tolerant
with the convictions of others,
willing to proclaim but just as willing to listen,
and ready always to reach out
to someone who is lost and lonely.
And while I am a servant may I be a student as well,
willing to learn and to grow
in my understanding of life
and your purposes in the world about me.

WHEN THE HOURS
ARE LONG AND TEDIOUS

I pray, my Lord,
that you will fill my hours of solitude
with a deep sense of your loving presence.
My job is lonely,
devoid of the excitement
of new faces and experiences.
The hours are long and tedious,
and sometimes the drudgery is intolerable.
Yet I am your child
and am in this place to carry on your purposes.
I dedicate even the dull and lonely hours
of my life to you, O Lord.
May they serve to accomplish your objectives
in me and through me.

THE NEED
TO PROVE SOMETHING

Sensitize me to your Spirit and your will, O God,
that I may ever be alert
to the opportunities that come my way
to witness in loving deed
and with enlightening word
concerning your gifts of grace and love.
Deliver me from the need to prove something
that I may focus on the privilege of manifesting you.
Keep me from manipulating and exploiting people
to gain credits for myself.
Set me free, O Lord, to freely, openly,
honestly, and lovingly represent
and reflect you
in my daily relationships.

I WANT SOMETHING
FOR MYSELF

O God, I am tired of the hard road,
the dusty valley,
the smog and noise of city streets.
My hands are dirty,
my feet are sore;
my heart is heavy with the concerns of others.
I'm fed up, O God.
I just can't take it any longer—
the scorn of the indifferent,
the snickers of those who take advantage of me,
the despair of failure in my dealings with men.
I want something for myself, O Lord—
to walk on water, to heal the sick,
or at least to receive a little appreciation,
to get a medal or a certificate of merit,
or even a commendatory slap on the back.
Give me some measure of success, O God,
some sense of importance,
some mountain on which to be transfigured,
some out-of-this-world experience
to give wings to my flagging spirit.
Forgive me, O God,
for these unworthy and unwarranted feelings.
May the crucible of this life purge me
of my lust for self-esteem
and render me effective as your servant.

IN DIFFICULT TIMES

WHEN I AM FRIGHTENED

O God, I know all the words
designed to comfort and assure.
I am aware of your promise to stay close beside me
whatever the crisis that confronts me.
But I am frightened, Lord,
and I cannot evade the anxieties that confront me.
Forgive me for my small faith
and large doubts, O Lord,
for finding it so difficult to really trust you
on the threshold of this fearful chapter in my life.
You have promised sufficient grace for special trials.
I lay claim to that grace
and pray that you will help me in some special way
to sense your loving presence
in undergirding and overseeing my life
in this time of testing.

WHEN FACED
WITH A TERRIBLE LOSS

I have suffered a terrible loss in my life, O God,
and want to believe that you really care.
You let it happen, Lord,
and I keep asking *why?*
But the skies remain cold and gray
with merciless silence.
I know I must accept it and learn to live with it;
but the vacuum, the emptiness,
the excruciating agony,
flatten me with despair.
Now, O God, fill in the vacuum,
absolve the emptiness,
resolve the bitterness,
enable me to endure the pain,
and help me to be so close to you
that I may be grateful for what you have given me
even if such gifts cannot remain mine forever.
Turn the ashes of my loss
into something beautiful and useful.
I can't do this, dear Lord, but you can.
Do it now, Lord; please do it now.

WHEN I AM INCAPACITATED

I have been incapacitated, my Lord,
and I am facing a long period of resting and waiting.
My normal responsibilities must be shelved,
or placed in the hands of others.
I can no longer do what I was trained to do
or care for those for whom I am responsible.
I do not see how my life can now be of any use
to you or my fellowman.
I pray, O God,
that you will care for those I cannot serve
and will fill in the empty spaces
caused by my absence.
Resolve the anxieties of my life
and grant that I may rest in your care and concern.
You have not given me up, O Lord.
Work out your purposes within me
and enable me to find some way
of serving you and others right here where I am.

WHEN FACED
WITH AN IMPORTANT DECISION

I am faced with an important decision, Lord,
and I am concerned that I find your will
in respect to the direction
you would have me to go.
You know my strengths and weaknesses, Lord,
and you know how and where I can best serve you.
You also know my needs, Lord,
and how foolishly I interpret them
and attempt to fulfill them in self-serving ways.
Break through my selfish desires and my endeavors
to build up my own ego;
set me free from these self-serving tendencies
that I may see and fulfill your will and purposes
in all things that affect my life and living.
Help me, Lord, to make my decision
not in terms of what it will do for me
or how much I may benefit by it,
but in terms of where I can most effectively
serve you and others about me.

WHEN AN ILLNESS
IS TERMINAL

I have been informed that my illness
may be terminal,
that there is nothing more
that medicine can do for me.
I suspected it for some time, O Lord,
and you have already been at work in my life
with special injections of grace.
Somehow, I am not afraid anymore.
I feel you are near; I sense your loving concern.
All life is terminal on this earth
but I really believe
that its end is only the beginning,
another important step in your creative process.
I am grateful, Lord,
that you are beside me all the way
and will accompany me in this new adventure
into regions and experiences
that are beyond human knowledge or comprehension.
Now, my God, I pray for my dear family and friends
who may not feel your nearness
as clearly as I do in this moment.
Grant them, also, your grace.
Their pain is far greater than mine.
Have your own way, Lord, with me and with them,
for we are yours forever.

THE LOSS OF A CHILD

You gave us the most beautiful gift
we have ever known, O God,
and then you took it away.
There are moments
when we wish we had never known
the joy of this precious gift,
this lovely child you entrusted to our care.
Maybe we were not worthy, God,
or faithful stewards of this charge
that you placed in our hands.
There are moments of bitterness, God,
when we are tempted to accuse you of cruelty,
when we dare to doubt your concern and your love.
And yet we know you to be a gentle Father
who forgives our yesterdays
and blesses our tomorrows
and who feels the very pain you permit us to endure.
We can only pray that you will enable us to feel
what we know we ought to express—
gratitude for the short time that
your child was entrusted to us,
for the supreme happiness that was ours together.
You have taken our child, O Lord.
Only you know the reason.
We thank you because we know he is yours forever.

THE LOSS OF A MATE

She was so precious to me, O Lord.
and now you have taken her from me.
Oh how I loved her, Lord, and needed her!
Next to you, I loved her more than anyone
or anything I have ever known.
There were times when
she was more important to me
than you and your purposes for my life.
And there were far more occasions
when I placed my selfish concerns
far ahead of my love and concern for her.
I pray that you will cover my guilt, O Lord.
She was your gift to me, my God,
without the guarantee that I could have her forever.
I am grateful, Lord—
even while my heart cries out in bitterness.
Forgive me that I cannot joyfully
commit her into your hands.
Nevertheless, I do so—reluctantly—
and I pray that your miracle-working grace
will put me together again,
that you will fill the empty places in my life,
and renew, encourage, and strengthen me.
She has left me, Lord, but you haven't.
Put my feet in motion again, O Lord,
that I may continue to walk in your paths
and carry on your purposes.

WHEN THE HOUR GROWS LATE

My God, my Guide, my Master and my Companion,
you have stayed close beside me
through more years than I care to count.
Through summers of joy and winters of discontent,
through springtimes of promise
and autumns of depression,
you have never left my side.
When I have fallen, you have picked me up.
When I recklessly walked the edge of ruin,
you were there to hold me back.
Even when I screamed in protest
and rebelled in disobedience,
your chastisement was gentle
and your love was constant.
Now it is getting late, O God,
and sometimes I feel resentful.
Forgive me for looking back, dear Lord,
except to glory in your presence and your care
throughout those perilous years.
I seek not to be younger in years
but to be young and ever vital in spirit.
Grant, my God, that your eternal Spirit
may replenish the dry wells of my life,
that even though my bones may ache
and my activities diminish,
my life may be a spring of living water
to my brothers and sisters about me.

WHEN FACING SURGERY

My doctor has ordered me into surgery, O God.
It will be one of the rare times in my life
when I will relinquish all rights, all self-control,
the very beat of my heart
into the hands of other human beings.
I am courting some apprehensions, my Lord.
I may manage to hide them from my loved ones,
but you know my fears
as I prepare to gamble with uncertainty
in the valley of shadows.
I don't have to be afraid.
You have promised to stay by my side.
I lay claim to your forgiving and sustaining grace.
I commit my loved ones—
and my own body and being—
into your loving care.
Whether I awaken to carry on
your purposes in this world
or enter into the eternal glory
of your ultimate destiny for me,
this is in your hands, dear Lord;
I am content to leave it there,
to pray that your will be done.

WHEN ONE LOSES
HIS JOB

There were times, O God,
when I claimed to believe your great promises
and insisted that my dependence was on you.
Now that the rug has been pulled out from under me
I find myself clawing for some tangible support,
some evidence of your concern for me
and for those who look to me for material security.
I have lost my job, O Lord,
and I honestly don't know where to turn.
I am anxious and fearful.
I feel as if the bottom has dropped out,
and I am left grappling with nothingness.
Restore, O God, my confidence in you.
I have prayed that your will be done;
now help me to believe
that you will answer that prayer,
that you will work out your will in my life,
that this apparent loss
may be a step toward something
even more important and productive
in the months and years before me.
I am yours, O God, and you will never let me go.
Have it your way, Lord,
and grant me the faith to believe
that your way is the best way.

WHEN IT'S DIFFICULT
TO LOVE

I have discovered, O Lord,
that despite my enthusiastic affirmations
and proclamations of your love for mankind,
there are some people I do not like very much.
I have no problem with those
who affirm and support me.
But when it comes to people who attempt to use me,
or have no use for me,
or who even have the audacity
to question my motives or criticize my actions,
I feel very little love or concern for them.
While you love and accept me as I am,
even when I fail you or cease to serve you,
I am not capable of loving and accepting
those who do not in some measure serve me.
Inasmuch as I fail to love, I do fail to serve you.
I am still basically selfish,
concerned primarily about my own
station and status in life.
Is it possible, Lord, that I have been using you
to fulfill my aspirations
rather than to discover wholeness and fulfillment
in submitting myself to your loving control?
Forgive me, O God, and teach me anew
the meaning of your great love,
and how to love and accept others
as you love and accept me.

WHEN I AM DISCOURAGED

I've had it, Lord.
I've honestly tried to serve you,
to love my neighbor,
to share myself and my possessions with him.
It seems, however, that wherever I go
I run into stone walls.
And the very people I reach out to help
turn against me.
I've been conned, derided, abused.
I'm at the end of my rope,
and I just can't take it any longer.
Is it really true, Lord,
that I am expected to be like Christ?
I know the answer, Lord.
It is this to which you have called me.
It is for this
that I have been redeemed and commissioned.
It is because of this hard road
along which you lead me
that you grant me strength to endure,
joy in the midst of suffering,
and the assurance of ultimate victory.
Pull me out of this deplorable pit, O Lord.
I don't belong here; I am your son and servant.
Teach me, O God, how to accept my status
and the validity and power that goes with it,
and to walk and serve in joy.

MY PLACE
IN A REVOLUTIONARY WORLD

I live, my God, within an ongoing crisis.
It is the crisis of revolution,
a rapidly-changing, churning, conflict-ridden world.
It is frightening at times.
My reaction is often a retreat
to the sanctuary of the past
where I assume I can be free
from the everyday tensions of this life.
I even look to my church
where I hear those great words
about my security and safety in you.
Nevertheless, you forbid, O God,
that I run away from this crisis.
You came to "set fire to the earth,"
and revolution is, in part,
a consequence of your Word to us.
You have placed me in the midst of crises, O God.
They are all about me.
Help me, undergirded by your grace,
filled with your Spirit,
to find my place in a revolutionary world,
to put my reputation, job, income, even my life
on the line to confront violence with courage
and hatred with love,
to be your faithful child and servant
in the midst of crises.

FOR SPECIAL PEOPLE

THANK YOU
FOR PEOPLE

Thank you for people, Lord,
short and tall, fat or small,
money-grabbers, pleasure-seekers, attention-getters,
the bold and the fearful,
the commanders and the demanders.
Some weep and whine; others curse and carouse.
Some are benign and some are belligerent.
Whoever they are, they are your creatures,
and you love them as you love me.
It is your will that I love them as well
and serve you through serving them.
It is so often through these very people,
whatever their exterior appearance,
that I see you reflected and hear you speak.
Rid me of self-concern, O Lord,
that I may be free and open
to your manifestations through others,
and that they may see you
reflected in my attitudes and actions.

THANK YOU
FOR MY FRIEND

I thank you for my friend, dear Lord.
You reached out through his devotion and concern
to kindle a new fire within me.
He broke through my apathy and depression
to reveal the beauty and fragrance of life about me.
He marched into my jungle of despair,
sliced through my confusion,
and gave order and motivation
to my purposeless gropings.
I am grateful, O God, to you and for him.
I pray that you would use me,
as you have so graciously used him,
to transmit joy to the joyless, despairing lives
of your children who cross my path.
And bless my friend, O God,
and keep him and use him forever.

A FRIEND
IN SERIOUS TROUBLE

I pray, O Lord,
for my friend who is in serious trouble.
He's blinded by the excitement of the moment, Lord,
and doesn't realize how much he is hurting himself
and his loved ones
by his actions.
He is a good man.
The last thing he would ever want to happen
is that he might bring hurt or harm
to someone else.
Deal gently with him, Lord,
but stop him before he goes too far.
Bring him back to the center of your will
and to the joy and purposefulness
that once marked the life and actions
of this one who is my friend.

THE MARRIAGE
OF FRIENDS

Our great and loving God,
whose eternal love has now united
our dear friends in the relationship of marriage,
grant them now and forever
the grace to live in accordance with your Word
and to follow together in your footsteps.
Sustain them in their faith and affection
toward each other;
watch over them and stay close to them
in all the trials and conflicts of this life.
Send them forth as your servants
to exemplify and demonstrate toward each other,
and in their relationships to other people
your great love for all humanity about them.
We commit them to your care, O God,
and pray that you will keep them forever.

FOR ONE
WHO IS VERY ILL

I am praying for my friend who is so very ill.
O my Lord, you brought the touch of healing
to those who crossed your path
in your earthly life.
You promised to respond to the prayers
of your children that struggle to follow
and reflect you on this earth.
Reach out now to this one with your healing touch.
She belongs to you, O God.
She yearns so deeply to serve you.
Restore her to life and wholeness once more.
And even while she suffers,
may she sense your nearness
and be embraced by your peace.
Grant that she may have joy
even in the midst of her sufferings.
And grant, blessed Lord,
that she might get well again.

ANOTHER FRIEND
WHO IS ILL

O Lord, you have often reached forth
to touch the fevered brow or the crippled body
with divine hands that bless and heal.
I pray for your healing touch
on the body of my dear friend.
I know not your will for him.
I cannot presumptuously claim
your healing on his behalf.
I can only seek to unite my loving concern
with your perfect and everlasting concern
and commit him into your loving care.
As precious as he is to me,
he is more precious to you, O God.
Whether his healing is revealed
in the visible deliverance from his malady,
or the invisible joy and strength and confidence
that will sustain and support him
even in the midst of his pain and conflict,
I can pray with confidence
that you will be close to him
and will accomplish your purposes
in and through him.
It is for this that I pray, my Lord.
Surround him with your love
and grant him your grace.

WHEN I'VE HURT SOMEONE

O my God, I've hurt someone deeply,
someone who trusted in me,
who thought I was strong and loyal and true.
In causing him pain I have caused you great pain.
I am so human, so frail, and so very foolish.
And I am sorry, Lord.
I would rather have died than let this happen.
But it has happened,
and I can only turn to you for forgiveness
and for restoration to you and your purposes.
I plead with you, my God, to heal his hurt.
My love, if it be love at all,
is selfish and distorted.
Your love is perfect and total and eternal.
Hold him close, O God,
and draw me back into your loving heart
and help me to love the way you love.

WHEN SOMEONE
HURTS ME

Someone stepped on me today, O Lord,
and I reacted in frustration and anger.
I guess I'm pretty fragile; I break so easily.
I am so completely dependent on the good wishes
and commendations of others.
Anyway, I did not act like your servant
but more like a spoiled child still grappling
for some sense of personhood or identity.
I have so much to learn, Lord,
especially about what it means to be your child
and to be your disciple assigned to relate
and to reflect you to the people about me.
Set me free, God,
from the need to be the king-of-some-hill,
even the need to be appreciated and respected,
and help me to find my joy and my measure of worth
in your love
and in my relationship to you.

SOMEONE
WITH A LARGE PROBLEM

I am praying, O Lord,
for someone who has a large problem.
He is your child and disciple,
the object of your love and concern.
And he is important to those around him.
He has been laid low with discouragement
and flattened by depression.
He feels that you are looking the other way
or are too busy with other things
to pay much attention to him.
And so he withdraws into himself
and grieves in his despair.
You know his needs;
I know only something of his misery.
You know how much he needs you,
that you are the answer to his deepest longings.
Draw him to yourself, O God.
Enable him to feel your touch of healing
on his crippled spirit.
Even in this moment,
help him to feel that you are near to him
and to see some flicker of light on his dark path.
Grant him your grace, O Lord,
for he belongs to you.

THANKS FOR MY FAMILY

I thank you, my God, for my family.
I pray that I may be faithful and responsible to them
even while I seek to be faithful to you.
Forbid, O God, that my love be confined
to them alone,
or that I selfishly possess
or exploit them for my own needs.
You and your purposes are primary.
There are others that I must love and serve
in the world about me.
Yet I must pray, O God,
that I do not neglect these who are dearest to me.
May our love for each other stretch our souls
and enlarge our capabilities to love people.
And may we all abide in your love forever.

WHEN AT ODDS
WITH MY MATE

I am at odds with my mate, O God,
and I can't believe that it's all my fault.
Yet I know that I have been guilty of trying
to impose my will and even my convictions on her.
I take her for granted and treat her at times
as if she belonged to me.
She belongs to you, O Lord.
You graciously share her with me,
but you forbid that I possess her for myself
or attempt to make her conform to my image.
As you set me free to be myself,
enable me to support and encourage
that gift of freedom for her.
Teach me how to truly love her,
to be close to her in her need
and yet not so close
as to stifle her in her growth,
to allow her to be what you want her to be
that she may be whole and happy
and may enrich the lives of others
even as she enriches and blesses my life.

THANKS FOR OUR CHILDREN

We have always been grateful, O Lord,
for our children,
the precious ones you have committed to our care.
We have, however, been fearful and anxious at times,
and sometimes irresponsible as their parents.
We have sought to possess them
and have used them to fill the emptiness of our lives
and sometimes to camouflage failures in our living.
We have found our joy in them
and exercised our hostilities on them.
Yet in our selfish way
we loved them and sacrificed for them,
wanting desperately that they be happy
and successful in the course of their lives.
We have failed at times
to recognize our stewardship, O Lord,
and have attempted to mould them in accordance
with our short-sighted and limited aspirations.
And we have often failed in our most important task
with these dear ones:
to demonstrate a loving commitment to you
and to the human family throughout the world.
Help us to live in such a way, dear Lord,
that our children will know that we have discovered
that real life and eternal joy
and ultimate worth and meaning come by way
of a loving and trusting relationship with you.

WHEN PRESENTED
WITH A CHILD

O God, you have blessed us
with a precious token of your love for us
and your trust in us as your servants.
And you have given to us
an awesome and fearful responsibility.
You have presented to us a lovely child.
Our hearts are almost exploding in gratitude.
Grant to us, loving Lord, the grace to believe
that with this gift is also given the strength
and the wisdom to faithfully
carry out our stewardship.
This delightful creature is your child, O God.
We are privileged to enjoy him,
and commissioned to share our lives with him
and to communicate your love and purposes to him.
We, by your grace, assume the responsibility,
and we pray that we may rear your child
in accordance with your will and design for his life.

AFRAID
FOR OUR CHILDREN

We are fearful for our children, dear Lord.
They are so continuously exposed
to the hazards of this life
and the atrocities of our world.
They are constantly under the influence of people
who do not feel as we do
about life's goals and objectives.
The value-system which we have tried to lay on them
is perpetually challenged by the society
in which they live and move.
O God, we can't shield them from the world
and its influences
or from life and its realities.
We continue to commit these dear ones to you
and pray that while we cannot
impose our values on them,
we can discover true life and purpose
in a relationship of love and trust in you
and demonstrate by our living the joy
of being your servants and disciples.
Grant, O God, that we may reflect you
rather than promote or program you
in the lives of our children.
Bless them, Lord, that they may belong to you
forever.

FOR AGED PARENTS

We pray, our great God, for our aging parents,
and for the elderly saints about us
who have retired from active service
to await your call to far better things.
We love these dear people,
but we so often neglect them
in our persistent grasp for recognition and security.
We take them for granted,
assuming their needs are met
and their desires fulfilled.
We are their offspring.
We are here because of the sacrifices and risks
they took on our behalf.
They were faithful servants, many of them,
and they communicated your love
and grace to our lives.
Bless them, O God, warm their hearts
with an intense feeling that you are near to them.
And help us, O God,
to see their needs,
to feel something of their loneliness,
and to be channels of your love and grace to them.

FOR OUR PASTOR

We pray for our pastor, dear Lord.
We can only guess about the pressures
that besiege him,
but we ought to be aware of his humanity,
his weaknesses and his strengths,
his need for human love and concern.
We know, as well, how easy it is for us
to expect superhuman feats from this man,
to assume that he has some special corner on you,
or some special grace or gift
that will enable him to meet all our needs,
calm our fears,
eliminate our conflicts,
and make for us a kind of heaven in this world.
You sent him to us in response to our prayers.
But you sent us a man, not a god,
with needs and wants equal to any man,
and with temptations and conflicts
that may be greater than those of most others.
Help us, our loving God, to love him, respect him,
confide in him, listen to him, be patient with him,
excuse and forgive him.
And help us, his co-ministers,
to assist him in advancing
your kingdom in our world.

CONCERN
FOR OUR CONGREGATION

Bless our church, O God,
and the many who make up our congregation.
We are obstinate and rebellious children
and often oblivious to the needs of one another.
You are patient with us, our loving God,
and you have not given us up.
Teach us how to love one another
and how to act like your loving sons and daughters
rather than jealous children fighting
for recognition and acceptance.
Draw us together in unity and strength
that the people of our community may see
that you are God and may sense through us
some measure of your love for them.

MY RELATIONSHIP WITH GOD

SEEKING FOR GOD

We cannot see you, O God,
even when there are reflections of your power
and presence all about us.
We have for too long been enamored with
cement and steel and plastic,
with small gadgets and great machines,
with tall buildings and wide freeways.
And we have for too long limited our worship
to rituals and words.
We sometimes feel as if we have been cornered
and trapped by the unreal and irrelevant.
Break into our dark cells, O Lord,
and bring us back to the reality of your glory
and beauty and majesty:
in the great mountains
that tower over our small achievements,
in the exquisite flower and the graceful tree,
in green hills
and sun-bathed plains
and thundering surf.
Free up our senses, Lord,
that we may see and hear
and feel and smell
the wonders of your world about us,
and assure us once again that you are
our almighty and everlasting God.

WHEN THE FIRE
BURNS LOW

This is the hour of worship, O God,
and I feel dull and lethargic.
My soul is as gray as fog.
I am numb, O Lord.
The inner fires have died out.
I hear and I read your words—
but they are just words.
Even the music that used to set my heart singing
is at this moment but weird sounds
going in different directions.
I just can't feel grace or respond to challenge.
I know you are somewhere about, my Lord,
that my feelings are no measure of your nearness.
But I need to feel good sometimes, O God.
Forbid that I pin my faith on what I may feel,
but grant some sense of your presence in this hour
that I may sing your praises
and worship you with joy.
Turn up the fire within me, dear God,
that my life might glow again
and the lives of others may be warmed through me.

THE NEED
FOR A VISION

My great God, I am still learning how to walk.
And I believe that you walk beside me
among the mundane, the ordinary,
even the relevant, nitty-gritty facts
of everyday living.
I know I can worship you
even as I walk through busy streets
and the frantic, tension-filled hours of the daily grind.
There are, however, times
when I need the feeling of soaring—
to see mountain-tops and colorful sunsets,
to hear majestic chorales,
to meditate on profound philosophies,
to mark that vertical dimension that turns my head
and my heart upward and beyond the dusty valleys
where men sweat and swear and struggle and suffer.
I ask not that you remove me from the valley,
or for escape or refuge.
I ask only that my heart and imagination be enriched
and inspired with visions
that transcend the commonplace
and that you grant to me the grace
to translate such visions into words and deeds
that will enrich my life as well as
the shallow lives of earth-bound men about me.

WHEN ONE HAS FAILED

I have failed again, O Lord.
Despite my firm resolutions and determined efforts,
I have flopped—fallen on my face.
It is difficult to believe, dear Lord,
that this does not come between me and you,
that you refuse to give me up,
that your grace is sufficient in spite
of the frailties and faults of my life.
It is thus that I fall only to rise again,
wounded in battle only to fight on another day.
And it is thus that I come limping back to you.
Forbid, O God, that I should ever be so broken and
beaten down that I fail to come limping back to you.
Pull me to my feet again, O God.
Grant to me the assurance of ultimate victory
that I may be strong and faithful
in my daily conflicts.

CLAIMING GOD'S GRACE

I have sinned against you, God,
and against my brother.
Because of my self-centeredness,
my grappling to meet my needs and satiate my senses,
to nullify my loneliness and boost my ego,
I have hurt someone that you love.
I can think of excuses, Lord,
my humanity, my weaknesses,
the circumstances under which I live and work.
You do not, however, accept my excuses;
you only offer me your grace.
Your grace is and always has been available.
I claim it anew, dear God.
Envelop me in your love,
and may it enable me to truly love,
the kind of love that will heal my brother's wounds
and bring to each of us joy and strength once more.

ACKNOWLEDGING
MY IDENTITY

I thank you, my great God,
for you made it possible for me to know who I am.
You have touched me with your cleansing power
and placed your Spirit in my heart.
I am your child
even while I am fallible and often very foolish.
I am your servant—and am to serve you
by serving my brothers and sisters about me.
I am redeemed by your love,
sanctified through your righteousness,
ordained by your calling, empowered with your grace
I am destined to represent your purposes
and to demonstrate and communicate your love
to those who cross my path.
Thank you, God, for making me
valid and significant,
for putting meaning and purpose into my life,
for snatching me out of the pit of self-centeredness
and restoring my identity as a member
of your eternal family.

FOR FAITHFULNESS

I know, O Lord, that I have always belonged to you.
I know, as well,
that I have often tried to run from you,
foolishly thinking that happiness and adventure
were somewhere out there with the bright lights
and the laughing crowd.
I feel a little lonely, Lord,
because so many of my friends
are not with me in faith
and do not know you as I do.
But I am thankful you led me
to the decision and the determination
to surrender my life to you and your purposes.
And my heart is filled with joy—
the kind of joy that bright lights
and laughing crowds
could never equal.
You are, O Christ, my Savior and my Master.
This is the way I want it—now and for always.
I know that I will not always feel close to you,
but I know that you will forever be by my side,
that I never need to be afraid
because you will never leave me.
Help me, O God, to be faithful to you,
to be your child and your servant wherever
you may lead me and whatever may be
the trials and tribulations that cross my path.

LOOKING ON THE CROSS

O God, I gaze on the cross
of your Son, Jesus Christ,
and discover in its terrible pain the joy and peace
of forgiven sin and the freedom to live
in loving relationships with my fellowman.
I discover, as well, that there is pain for me,
that I am destined to be another Christ,
that there are crosses for me to bear
in my journey through life.
It is this to which you have called me.
It is for this
that I have been redeemed and commissioned.
It is because of this hard road
along which you lead me
that you grant me strength to endure,
joy in the midst of suffering,
and the guarantee of final victory.
I thank you, my loving God,
that you who brought the promise of life
to all men through the cross of Christ,
will turn the small crosses of my life
into agents of redemption and channels of love
to those whom I may touch
on my pilgrimage through this world.

YOU ARE HERE, LORD

O God, sometimes I am frightened
by the insecurities about me.
I am sorely tempted to run for my life,
to take refuge in some foolish escapade
that dims the vision or drugs the soul.
But you are my place of refuge, O Lord.
You are here,
and you are aware of my fears and apprehensions.
You can transform my fears into a faith
that will draw me closer to you
and serve to perform your purposes in my life.
I thank You, God, because you are here in my world.
Even among the difficult circumstances
that plague my life
I know I can find my security in you.

PRAISE AND THANKS

PREPARING FOR CHRISTMAS

We could not find you, our loving God,
so you have sought us out.
Prepare our hearts so we may recognize anew
the eternal significance of your coming to us
through your Son, Jesus Christ.
You have come, O Lord, and you continue to come
into the hearts of all those who are open
to you and your will for their lives.
May your coming to us give us strength
in our many conflicts
and throw light
on the dark paths that we must travel
in our disjointed and violent world.
Make us ready for this season of celebration
that we may receive you and serve you forever,
and make us the vehicles and messengers
of your gifts of grace
to the hearts and lives of others.

GOD HAS COME

Great God, you have come to us.
You have made yourself known
to our world through your Son.
You came by way of the stable and the manger
and the womb of a woman.
And you came to be my Savior and my King.
I have seen the light.
I have heard the Word
that announced the great event,
the glorious happening of your coming to us.
You have broken through
the distortions and darkness of sin
to prepare a way of salvation for all men.
Enable me now, O God, to follow
that One you have sent
and thereby to discover
the joys of your love and grace.
O God, you have come,
and now I shall praise you forever.

GOD IS HERE—
LET'S CELEBRATE

You are here, O God; you are now!
It is time for celebration!
Your promises have been proclaimed
throughout the ages.
With voice and musical instruments,
with lovely melodies and joyful sounds,
your name has been heralded
and your great words celebrated.
Now it is our turn to worship you,
to announce your presence and loving concern
for the inhabitants of this world.
Help us, O God, to fill our homes and sanctuaries
our halls of learning, our offices of government,
our streets and marketplaces,
with the glad, joyful sounds of celebration.

AN EPIPHANY PRAYER

Eternal God, we cannot see the star
that led the Wise Men to the birthplace of your Son,
but we can know by faith your presence
and power in our lives.
The Jesus who was born in Bethlehem
can be born anew in us
and can live in and through us
who inhabit the world of today.
It has happened, O Lord.
You abide within us, and you go before us.
Whatever may befall us on our course
through this fractured world,
may we follow unafraid,
and faithfully carry out your purposes
in scorn of consequences.

CHRIST IS ALIVE

You are alive, O Christ; you are for real!
You have overcome death once and for all!
You have demonstrated your great power
in rising from the grave.
How foolish I have been in doubting such power
in the midst of my small problems
and many frailties!
Now I know once more
that nothing that may confound
or perplex me is too great for you.
I pray, O God,
that the power that raised Christ from the dead
may raise me out of my fears and failures
to share in that great resurrection
and to celebrate forever
your victory over sin and death.

WHEN EASTER
HAPPENS TO US

Our loving God,
you who raised Jesus Christ from the dead.
Lest this divine miracle be in vain,
show us how the power of the resurrection
can be applied to our personal lives.
Raise us from our graves of defeat and despair
and send us forth to reflect and to demonstrate
your resurrection power to others
in our world about us.
Touch others through us, O God, with that power,
that they may be raised from the dead
to live and serve and praise you forever.

PRAISING GOD

I praise you, O God.
As long as I have breath in my body,
I will praise you.
You created the earth and all that abides on it.
You can heal the wounds and mend the fractures
of this disjointed world.
You can break the bonds of man's obsessions
and pierce his stupor with visions of truth.
You tenderly reach out to those who are oppressed
and reveal your concern
for those who are lost and lonely.
You watch over your own,
and you love them and care for them.
I praise you, O God,
for truly you are a great God.

GOD IS WITHIN US

O God, you took your Son
from our midst only to return
to us by way of your invisible Spirit.
Enable us, though we cannot see you
and even when we cannot feel your presence by way
of some mystical, supernatural experience,
to know that you dwell within us
and are here with us in our fellowship together.
May your Holy Spirit so abide in our hearts
and guide our activities
that we may walk in your paths for us
and accomplish those things
you would have us to do.
Thank you, Lord, for coming to us,
for the gift of your Spirit,
for redeeming us and commissioning us
to be your children and your servants,
your vessels and vehicles,
in the extending of your kingdom
in this world about us.

FROM GRIPING
TO GRATITUDE

My loving God,
you have turned my griping into gratitude,
my screams of despair into proclamations of joy.
How can I help but explode with praises
and vow to spend eternity in thanksgiving to you?
You are my hope and salvation,
the morning sun and the evening star,
my shade in the desert heat,
my warmth in the cold of the night.
You are the Bread of Life,
and life-giving springs
when my soul is parched and dry.
You are the answer to my agonizing questions,
the fulfillment of my deepest longings.
I am yours, O God, yours forever.
Make my life a perpetual offering of praise.

HE DOES
ALL THINGS WELL

I proclaim your name
and shout your praises, my God.
You draw me into the crucible of conflict.
You test and try me in the valley of sorrow.
You allow me to taste the agony of affliction.
You even allow my peers to oppose and oppress me.
And then you use these very things
to purge and prepare me for your purposes.
So I shout your praises, O God,
for you do all things well,
and I know that you will love me forever.

IN A TIME OF ECSTASY

Never, O Lord, have I felt your nearness
as I have today.
It has been a "burning-bush" experience,
a "Mount-of-Transfiguration" episode in my life.
My every human sense and faculty was immersed
in the beauty and power of your presence.
I felt as if I might explode with joy.
O Jesus, you were so real, so precious, so close to me.
Why, my God, can't I always feel this way?
I know I must leave the mountain top
to run your errands and serve your children
in the valley.
You must help me to understand
and to believe, O God,
that while the feelings of your nearness may
dim or diminish,
the fact of your presence is forever secure.
You are always near.
You are with me and you will go before me
even amidst the tragedies and dark crises
that clutter my course through life.
Thank you, O Lord, for surprising me with joy.
May it refresh and recharge
my life and my faith in you.
May it resolve in a deeper dedication
to your purposes,
and bring some joy to the lives of others
who cross my path.

PRESENTATION OF A CHILD

It is with pride and with joy
that we bring our child to you, our Lord.
We honor and praise you, O God,
as we dedicate this precious life to you.
We know that he belongs to you,
that your Spirit abides within him,
that we, child and parents,
are really brothers and sisters
within the family of God.
How grateful we are for your confidence in us,
for the privilege and responsibility
of shepherding him through the years
of childhood and youth!
We claim your grace and your wisdom
for this awesome task.
Help us to be faithful in our assignment.
And bless and keep our young one
that he may someday hear your call to service
and take up his cross to follow you.

PREPARING
FOR HOLY COMMUNION

We praise you, our Lord,
for the prophets and apostles
who brought your eternal Word to us,
and for those who proclaim and minister that Word
to our needy spirits.
We praise you, O God, for your Son, our Savior,
the Word made flesh for our sakes and our salvation.
And we give thanks because you are aware
of the human condition and of our need
to more tangibly experience that Word
through Holy Communion.
We have recognized our wrong doings
and embraced your forgiving and accepting grace.
Now we pray that we may sense in a very real way
your loving presence and your healing touch
on our bodies and spirits.
Come to us, O Christ,
by way of the bread and the cup,
and by way of loving fellowship with
other members of your body,
to increase our faith, renew our courage,
and deepen our commitment
to you and your purposes
in our world.
Come, O Lord, and give us
your grace to truly love one another.

NATION AND WORLD

LOVE FOR COUNTRY

We love our country, O God.
The acquisition of our land
has not always been honorable.
Our treatment of the minorities
has been inexcusable.
Our selfish utilization of the land's resources
is deplorable.
Yet there is so much beauty;
and where your precepts have been practiced,
light and liberty have pushed back the shades
of darkness and oppression.
We love our country, O God.
Teach us how to love its people—your people—
and how to share its rich treasures with all
your children whatever their race or creed
or point of origin.
Protect us from our enemies, O God,
those enemies that threaten from within,
our apathy, our insensitivity, our self-centeredness
and bigotry.
Help us to keep our country, O God,
and to make it a secure and happy sanctuary
for all who dwell within it.

HEALING OF OUR LAND

Heal our land, O Lord.
We are not what we expected to be
or what you wanted us to be.
When men turn away from you,
they turn against one another.
There are poverty and oppression
and lawlessness and corruption.
Even many of our leaders have recited worthy creeds
while they sought personal goals
of wealth and power.
Give to us men and women
who will courageously seek and speak the truth
and who will dedicate their lives and their leadership
to the welfare of all the inhabitants
of our great country.
We are sick, O Lord, even unto death.
Heal our land, O Lord.

CARE FOR THE EARTH

Our world is beautiful and bountiful, O Lord.
It is because this is your world, your creation,
and you have appointed and empowered us
to be your co-creators as well as your caretakers
of this beautiful planet.
We have harnessed great rivers
to provide for man's daily needs,
and we have polluted them with our wastes.
We have turned barren lands into green parks,
and we have despoiled them with our carelessness.
We have carved up our valleys, stripped our forests,
depleted our soil, and even filled the very air
that we breath with suffocating impurities.
We have selfishly possessed this earth for ourselves
and extracted from its vast treasures more
than was due us
and more than we needed to sustain us.
Appointed to create, we have chosen to abuse,
and even while we call ourselves your children,
have vandalized and all but destroyed the home
you made for us.
We seek your forgiveness, O God,
and your wisdom to care for our earth
and to be faithful stewards over that
which you have entrusted to us.

THOSE WHO SERVE
IN OUR WORLD

We pray today for those who serve in difficult places.
We offer our gratitude to you for those
who man front-line positions,
who are committed to demonstrating and proclaiming
your eternal love in circumstances
and conditions where your Word and objectives
are not acclaimed or applauded.
We follow them with our prayers, O Lord,
that you would encourage and inspire,
comfort and sustain them in their service
to you and to your children.
Their successes are often not obvious
and cannot be measured by worldly standards.
There are pitfalls and precipices all about them.
There are powerful men and movements that are
hostile to them and to you and your purposes.
They are your children and your servants.
Grant them oases along their desert paths,
springs of water along steep and rocky trails,
and the joy and satisfaction of knowing that
they are close to your heart and are walking
obediently in your course for their lives.
Grant, O Lord, that they be faithful to you,
and that we might be faithful to them,
in praying and loving and supporting and in sharing
with them your gracious gifts to us.

THE POOR AND OPPRESSED
OF OUR WORLD

It is easy, O God,
to mouth my concern for this world's
oppressed and deprived peoples.
I pray that your love for me
will generate a genuine concern
for the suffering and dispossessed of the earth.
They are your children, Lord,
and they are my sisters and brothers.
They, too, constitute the body of Christ.
When one member suffers, the whole body suffers.
Even while I rejoice in your saving grace,
enable me to feel the hurt and to share
in the pain of other people.
Grant that I may be loving enough to share
with them your gifts to me
and wise enough to discover ways of communicating
to them your eternal concern and love.

PEACE IN OUR WORLD

O Lord, you never guaranteed that we would
have perpetual peace in our disjointed world.
As we have used the fortunes of war for selfish ends,
so we, for the most part,
will turn the years of peace into opportunities
for self-service and personal gain.
But it need not be so, O God.
On behalf of the masses who have suffered
so terribly and for so long,
we dare to pray for world peace.
We pray, as well,
that a time of peace may be a time of opportunity
to demonstrate and to communicate true peace
to the scarred and wounded spirits of your children.
We pray once more that swords will be
beaten into plowshares,
that people of all races may commune and share with
and care for one another,
and that every human creature may learn about
that peace that is beyond understanding
and which joyfully relates them to a loving God.

THE THINGS
OF THE WORLD

You have been so very good to me, O Lord.
My adversities have been small,
and your gifts have been abundant.
While I am grateful for these tangible gifts,
I have been threatened by the tyranny of things
and have often yielded to the temptation
to possess them for myself.
I lay claim to your forgiving love
and pray for the grace to yield them back to you
and for the wisdom to use these things entrusted
to my care for the accomplishment of your purposes
in the world about me.
I am your appointed steward, O Lord.
Lest the things of this world stifle and choke out
my relationship to you,
teach me, in response to your love,
how to make them work for you—
and how to fashion them into ways and means
of enriching the lives of others.

IN THE EVENING

IT'S BEEN A GREAT DAY

It's been a great day, Lord!
When I least expected it, I met you.
Forgive me for not anticipating your presence
in the people who cross my path.
Thank you for touching me with loving concern
in spite of my apathy and doubt,
for revealing yourself even through the gentle words
and actions of that one who,
though he didn't realize it,
lifted me out of my depression and self-pity
and put hope and joy into my life again.
Bless him, O God.
And make me that kind of person who will reflect
your joy in the midst of this world's loneliness
and communicate your love and peace to anxious,
weary, confused, unhappy,
hate-filled hearts about me.
Then tomorrow will also be a great day,
and I will celebrate your presence wherever I go.

I TRIED TO RUN AWAY

Dear Jesus,
I know that you never left me today,
but I'm afraid I tried to run away from you.
Instead of following you, I tried to lead the way.
I took things into my own hands,
and I ended up hurting those I wanted to help.
O God, I struck out; I failed; I lost the game.
Forgive me, Lord,
and make even out of the ashes of my errors
something that will be pleasing to you.
I meant well, Lord, but I performed so poorly.
Teach me how to rest in your will,
to wait for your guidance,
and to speak and act in gentleness and love
whatever the circumstances or difficulties
of each day.

YOU NEVER LEFT
MY SIDE

I thank you, my loving God,
because whether I win or lose,
I am secure in my relationship to you.
You may not have gone along
with everything I did today,
but you stayed with me and never left my side.
I didn't see you around every corner.
There were long hours during which I never
even thought about you.
And yet I knew you were close to me.
Thank you, Lord,
for the sweet assurance that you love me,
that I belong to you,
that you will never let me go.
I do not fear the night or the morrow.
Even if tomorrow never comes,
I rest in the arms of your forgiving love,
for I am yours forever.

THANK YOU
FOR THE NIGHT

Thank you for the night, dear Lord,
for the rest and the peace
that displaces the panic and frustration of the day,
and the time to mend life's ragged edges
and to refocus the heart and mind on those things
that are truly important.
And thank you for your word of forgiveness,
for the assurance of your love,
and the knowledge that as I rest my weary body,
I rest my spirit in your tender care.
Thank you, God,
that even before I lapse into unconsciousness,
I can discover anew my identity as your child,
and should I awaken to the morrow,
will begin a new day of challenge and opportunity
as your child and your servant.
Thank you, Lord.

WHEN I AM LONELY

I am lonely, Lord.
It is not the absence of people
that causes my complaint;
they have bustled by me throughout the day.
It is the absence of love and concern.
They would pause momentarily if they could use me.
They were even willing at times to abuse me.
Not one, Lord, not one was honestly concerned
about my feelings or my needs,
or appeared to regard me any more
than an animate object.
Forgive me, Lord, for wallowing in self-pity.
You have also walked the path of loneliness
and found comfort in the love of our Father.
It is true, O Lord, that even while I am lonely,
I am never alone.
I commit myself to your loving care this night,
and pray that on the morrow
I may not waste pity on myself,
but seek to express it in valid terms
of loving concern for those equally lonely people
who bustle by me throughout the day.

PICK UP
THE BROKEN PIECES

It has been one of those days, O Lord,
that I wish had never happened.
I've been zapped, squashed, beaten down!
It wasn't at all like the kind of victorious living
I had anticipated would be my lot as your servant.
I'm sorry, Lord, that I am so inept,
so foolish and clumsy
in my attempts to carry out your purposes.
There are, however, some days
in which nothing seems to work,
when everything I touch falls apart,
when I could have just as well stayed in bed.
May I entrust even these days
into your hands, O God?
Is it possible that you can make something
out of them that I could not?
I submit to you—not victories—but ashes.
Pick up the broken pieces of this day, O Lord,
and rework them
into something of value and significance.
And let me rest in the peace of your loving pardon.
and, if it be your will,
to rise to a new day
with renewed courage and confidence.

THE DAY IS OVER

The day is over, O God,
and I commit its failures
as well as its successes
into your hands.
I rejoice in your tender care
and celebrate your loving presence.
I pray that you will heal the wounds
of those I have hurt
and enrich the lives
of those I have helped.
I place in your care those I love the most
and those through whom
you ministered to me this day.
Bless them and keep them and fill their lives with joy.
I pray that you may somehow reach those whom
I couldn't love or make to feel my love,
that other of your faithful servants
may relate your concern for them.
Grant that I may truly learn how to love
as you love me
and to demonstrate that love to lonely,
despairing people in my path.
This day is over, O God,
its blessings and conflicts and disappointments.
If it be within your will, grant me another,
and help me to live it within your orbit
and your plan for my life.